Conduit

Sarah Frost

Conduit

Sarah Frost

Publication © Modjaji Books 2011

Copyright © Sarah Frost

First published in 2011 by Modjaji Books P T Y Ltd

P O Box 385, Athlone, 7760, South Africa

modjaji.books@gmail.com

http://modjaji.book.co.za

ISBN: 978-1-920397-27-2

Editor: Joan Metelerkamp

Book and cover design: Jacqui Stecher

Author photograph: David Glassom

Printed and bound by Mega Digital, Cape Town

Set in Walbaum

With thanks to Kobus Moolman, Liesl Jobson, Sally Ann Murray, Colleen Higgs, Moira Richards and Joan Meterlerkamp. I am also grateful to the University of KwaZulu-Natal English Department, whose Honours module in Creative Writing served me well.

For Gloria

Seahorse

Once,
I curled like a seahorse
on a whispering floor;
clear careful script
filling a secret book –

Time, a numb wave
surged over me. Twenty-two
times I nearly drowned;
found myself
floating.

Frieze

I swim to see sun
settle, clear as feeling, snake
skin helix sliding

down the pool — reaching
under would be nothing but
animating light.

Tree-fan

Homeward road — barren
as the winter tree fanning
small bones of branches.

Grahamstown

On the slopes the charred spines of the winter pines.
The town still in the valley below,
a pulse just visible in the soft hollows of a skull.

Lonely the forest road billowing sunset-red
for a girl on her bicycle, going home.

For her there can be no leaving, yet. Nothing to find.
Just a waiting as gradual as the evening train
shunting its heavy load free of the station.

Bed time, and the wind chime jangles.
Beyond the glass, a planet stark against the sky.

Restless, she turns under her covers at dawn,
hearing a truck shift down to its lowest gear.
The deep engine roar judders on the highway, departing.

No Purchase

No purchase,
the girl can find no hold.
All around her
fires are burning.
Dark landscapes
flit across the corner of her eye.

She remembers her mother
—— the cold from the earth
beneath her feet
seeps into her bones.

Her father is hidden from her.
Would she cut off
her right hand to find him

Above her
the starry sky
wheels.

Unknown birds lilt
from the strange night-time forest,
groundwater oozing through roots.

Her loneliness a torn coat,
she bares her breast
to a heartless moon.

Moths

Sudden as a gust of wind,
the moths flutter up from the hedge;
hundreds of them — brown, uniform.

She thinks that maybe
their wings are coated with poison
like the fragrance of hidden oleander,
sweetened by evening.

They cannot hear her
for her voice is softer than darkness,
dissenting.

Winter

The needy wind
skirls among the leaves –

an angry girl,
she sweeps her ragged skirt
across a patch of lawn.
She would make a haughty exit,
but the rusted gate snags her.

The lone palm frond
catches against the bars.

A jungle gym leaches
into the brittle strelitzia.

There is no escape
from this dying season.

A milkwood sees the paucity,
but offers no solution.
It cannot summon rain.

ii

Passing through

His eyes are holograms,
his body barely there,
in the darkness
beneath the lintel.

Passing through, into the courtyard
where children play,
trees fringe the lattice work.
A silvery summer sky yearns.

The lemon juice is bitter
before he adds sugared water.
It cools her mouth,
like a breath, close to the nape, flickers.

The febrile leaves of poplars
undulate in the air.
He kisses her solemnly
holding her close, at a distance.

Bellwood

She drives past bulls behind fences
to reach the cottages that
sit primly at the water's edge.

Purple flowers decorate the dry hillside,
amethysts around a sun-burnt neck.

A pin oak extends delicately
towards the sky. Horses mull.

Earlier, on the open road, her car flanked a train
as it probed the landscape, like a man entering a woman.

On her stereo, Alanis Morisette's lyrics blare
The words summon his face like an avatar:
sad clear eyes, thin-lipped mouth, jutting nose
swimming up in her mind like insistent fish.

Hours later, drunk, she leaves the birthday party,
to walk to where she will sleep that night
and lies on her bed, listening to the sounds of frogs
calling out across the water.
Laughter floats in through her open window,
like a half-drawn breath.

She remembers his words about her poems:
earnest, direct, removed.
Offering structure, a skeleton beneath flesh.

She scrawls in her notebook as a swimmer, fearful, under water
might search the opacity for a handhold, the roughness of rock.
She writes tentatively, as one standing up, walking to shore
might feel mud and soft lake moss beneath her feet, yielding.

Imago

From the hotel room on the twelfth floor,
I see windows from the city buildings
like clear eyes trawling darkness.
My host, boyish, told me earlier
of watching pigeons wheel here in the day,
their sounds muted by the air-conditioning unit.

Now, the noise is writers' talk, just back from the festival,
the radio journalist from Jozi on the edge of the bed,
speaks of being raped by a powerful man and how it felt when
no-one believed her. Next to her the sad solid editor
from the Kenyan slums, listening. In the corner I am drinking
whisky straight from the cool mouth of the Bell's bottle.
The lanky Ethiopian novelist sprawled across a chair
sips from a glass he found in the bathroom,
his eyes tender and wild as the desert he has left behind.

A light at the bedside table stands tall,
casting shadow like a sheet across the bed,
where he will dream that night. I wonder
why I want his attention. It is not just that
want burns, an inferno, inside my belly,
it is the wound of my history, one I cannot staunch.
He hands me a joint, the taste as elusive
as the goodbye graze of his stubble,

when later his kiss chastens,
a razor blade across my cheek, turning away.

Day

As the day, a mango,
sheds its skin
orange light snakes through the wild ginger leaves.

I want to take your loneliness,
I let your body dip into mine
as if I were the sea, and you the swimmer.

See how the clouds are clustered,
seeded with shadows.
They are ready to break open with love.

And the day comes.

Respite

The clouds this high afternoon
are children paddling in a dam at dusk,
the water pooling around their ankles.

On the ground the city is a gridlock
of roads and houses longing
for the heat to lift.

A storm might come
and light spills like semen
across the soft feathering morass that
keeps the dark at bay.

Thunder thrums;
the clouds hold back
like a woman, waiting.

Café Neo

So there we sat on the wooden deck,
with two red-winged starlings
and the mist rolling in from the rocks.

I pushed my full bag
under the spindly chair,
forcing it to give nothing away.

You showed me your website,
brimming with complexities;
brushing dust from the laptop screen.

I held the Windhoek lager coolly erect;
your green eyes sized me up
through the combatative clink.

You pointed out the lighthouse, explaining how it beams code
to the ships beyond Robben Island,
warning them of danger on the reefs.

We ate olives,
dipped warm pita bread in hummus,
tried the tzatsiki.

Your voice hummed like a ship's engine,
as you showed me a photograph of your mother,
her face wry with an unknown sadness.

You signed the bill,
carefully, as if writing poetry.
We kissed goodbye.

For the first time

She thought it would be different,
as outside the cicadas rubbed wings
in a frenzied call for a mate.

Instead, in his dark corner room
they tangled, antagonists. Her body,
taken, unheld, shrilled.

In this dusky place,
he left her all alone.

His mouth distant, hot, on her neck —
savage, in what she had hoped
would be their closest embrace.

Stranger

We are near the stage, our chairs adjoining.
My ankle rests on my opposite knee.
He slips his hand into my shoe,
to cradle the arch of my foot.

I wonder if he is thinking of the womb of our bed,
how last night he lifted the underneath of my leg
the better to push himself deep into me.
How my body received him, gratefully.

Delicate fingers
through the rough weave of the chair,
recall another man, another theatre.

My heart, a book, blows open,
my lover a storm of sentences,
but the pages driven back to the stranger's story,
half-lived, waiting for an ending.

Ménage-à-trois

The capsicum pot-plant tilts,
as you carry it precariously,
speaking of your wife, and how you owe her flowers.

Carting my own star-jasmine tethered to a wooden stick
to where we parked — we came separately —
I feel the cake we shared at the café above the nursery,
sit heavy in my stomach like woe.

You turn your car around and with a careful wave,
drive off, leaving me, hot-faced, heavy —
scrabbling to collect the coins that just fell out of my purse
into the gravel in the gutter.

Like a CD track stuck
the old song reverberates in my head

'the girl at the window/
waited all day for her father to come home/
thought that if she flirted with him/
he might love her more.'

At the table beneath the spreading fig tree,
I let you see my black bra-strap slip
from behind my green-yoked dress.
Felt your glance stroke my hair,
as you told me about paying your bond (and hers).

Your dessert fork glinted in the dappled light,
itching to wound.
My serviette, smeared red,
crumpled on a side plate.

iii

Looking glass

The bed below the midday window nests in sun.
He angles the mirror on the bureau opposite,
its cool surface showing the mess of their heat.

'Look,' he says, 'see how beautiful you are.'
His hands guiding her to touch her breasts, her belly,
round as a Zulu pot made from earth.

She splays for him,
the man's need like the deep fragrance of plants,
hovering over her skin.
He retrieves her mouth, his kiss a claiming.

Blanket

Her body still heavy
from being home to a baby for nine months
holds her feelings like a basket,
full of knitting.

From these skeins of wool,
some dark with grief for independence lost,
some blood-bright with remembered pain,
many glowing with joy

she makes a tangled throw
rough at the corners.

Later, she uses it to cover the child
sleeping in the centre of the marriage bed,
as his father, intimate, unknown, edges into her from behind,
awkward, displaced.

One year in

We argue all night, until I ask you to leave.
The next day we walk along the promenade.
I want to view the sea between trees, but
you pull me back, showing me wild jasmine.

We find a bench on the dune.
Below us, a family; a woman
smears sun-cream onto a man's face.
A brother and sister build a sandcastle.

You want this. For us, you've said.
I know I must relinquish my other search,
a father I have lost and survived;
but still the longing, an ache in the throat.

The sun glares, and waves barrage the beach.
I watch the small girl wrap her legs
around her daddy's waist, a limpet, not letting go.

Glimpse

At the dam that Christmas day
the father takes a digital photograph, and shows it to her,
offering a rare view of tenderness.
The boy combing out his mother's hair
as she throws her head back, glossy as a sunbird, and laughs.

Later, they walk to the valley's edge
and it's her turn with the camera.
Wild fuschia frames the father, a stoic Buddha,
cross-legged on a rock, boy in lap,
staring down the wind.

They tell him the story of how the valley was formed:
years of steadfast water erosion, the river below
snaking greenly towards the sea.
Trees chart its sibilant progress.

No longer together, joined forever
the man and woman follow their child running
through a field of yellow flowers, rising, tethered.

He leads them into the wattle stands, singing.

Graph

After all the nights you left me in a room with the baby
to sleep elsewhere
and only the wind shifting through the curtains,
to drown out the disconsolate sea.

After following the furniture truck to my own place and
breast-feeding on the floor, too sick to unpack the boxes;
this on the day you put your dog down,
her untreated wound teeming with maggots.

After all the sorrow, and I have not forgotten
how you placed my hand on our son's head
as he crowned between my legs
and how you held me through the pain.

Your mother died, and you flew to England
to burn her body; we took you to the airport
your boy, a dancing heart and I, a survivor.
I touched your shoulder in the departures hall.

This is love. A continuum
arcing in a trajectory of loss.
And we follow it unknowing
towards an indefinite end.

Threshold

From the bar at the pier's end
they saw the moon's pale hands
play across the sea as if it were a piano,
phrasing waves into a nocturne.

He held his beer glass
steady on the high counter,
as a breeze blew, and her shawl tassels
fluttered against her mouth.

She'd got a raise, she told him.
He was glad, he said.
She watched the night fisherman
step into the shallows, cast his line.

City lights felt the sky, found
the crescent of the bay,
completing the slow curve of ships
moored in the deepwater.

Along the beach
small ordinary fires
warmed the dark.

This side of the bay

Sunday morning, I distort.
A plant deprived of light etiolates.
The sky blares blue; cold as a blind eye.
palimpsest of the times years ago,
I was left alone, a frozen girl, unseen.

You walk with us on the Durban promenade.
The waves fall hard, far, there at the breakwater.
On this side of the bay, the sea is quiet as cobalt.

My child and yours ride bikes beneath the palms.
A sand-dredger moves methodically between the pier walls.
Later you leave to meet your wife and her sister somewhere
in town.

My son and I anchor a dome tent with beach stones,
it protects us from the bite of the winter wind.

You stroked my face

The Southern Cross, like a spoon
dips into the city bowl
scoops up the harbour lights,
the distant rattle of ships leaving,
freight trucks returning.

A fruit bat swoops into branches,
elusive as an unanswered question.

Saying goodbye, the man I want
so much it makes me silent,
kisses my face on both sides,
then turns away, shouldering the night.

Indoors, I lay my restless son down to sleep,
my fingers stroking love across his face.
I recollect the way you, my father, traced my forehead so,
when I was a child, when you held me during storms.

My tears prickle like dry grass against a bare foot
for what came later; for what you did not do,
for the leaving, and the staying away.

Sunday afternoon, birthday party

The clear-eyed child in her father's arms,
plump as a bubble,
floats into her second year.

The adults are there to welcome her,
their offspring clustered around them,
pawpaws on a tree.

The afternoon is moist as watermelon,
seeded with desire.
Its juice lingers like a song.

The guest
feels the sweetness of baklava
ache into her teeth.

She is thinking about loss
and ever-present others.
How tangled she is,
yet how free.

The mother, who a year ago was full with daughter,
watches, solemn as one of Vermeer's women,
her sadness inexplicable
as her longing to give birth once more.

Bearing

The woman, your friend, the one who has a name like yours,
her body shapeless after labour and breastfeeding:
she meets you in the street, not quite by accident.

It is an ordinary Tuesday afternoon, late.
Dogs sound off at each other,
like neighbours, testing limits.

Her older son pushes the pram
in which the baby sits
arms waving in disconnect.

Your dog strains at its leash,
disregarding your commands.

She takes him by the collar, holds him back
as she tells you of the test results.
From her mouth fall
the burnt seeds of words, like tumours.

Chaise longue

I recline —
sip lap sang souchong
from a cracked Delft mug,
brown, like river water
it tastes of smoke.

The window behind me empties
into a pool of roses.
Peonies spill onto soft grass.
The summer is insistent,
only the thin pane of glass keeps it at bay.

I half wish for curtains to draw
against the white light that striates my paper-thin skin.

The quiet of the house
descends like a Cy Twombly wave
thick, green and languid.

A crumpled lily leans from its vase,
submitting to a reflection
on the polished mahogany table.

Abahlali

They were the Abahlali, shack-dwellers,
their breaths misting the windows.
The rusted corrugated iron roof
nailed down their songs.

It was warmer in the hall.
Outside, the cold night air lay heavier
than water over shacks that tracked
a dirty sluice downhill.

She was Nomvuyo, Vusile's child, from the Eastern Cape.
Their Xhosa tongues clicked.
They took wood and plastic where they found it,
made their homes bordering eThekwini, in the 'mjondolo'.

Her father's eyes shone in the candle-light.
Men entered, their sjamboks overturning chairs.
'Kennedy Road for the Zulus,' they cried,
voices rising like hadedas in the night air.

Nomvuyo wrapped her blanket around her body,
and ran out where the door had been.
The police cars did not come.
People scattered, a handful of dust, thrown.

Angry men ransacked her father's home.
They tore a prayer-poster from the wall,
left a strand of plastic flowers dangling, displaced.

Now Nomvuyo begs for change,
at the robots on the M41.
The Umsinsi trees hide her when she sleeps,
their red flowers raging.

Conduit

For how long now
it has been blocked.
The tunnel full of ragged plastic bags, dead branches
washed down from the townships.
The water tainted with faeces.

Stagnant as oil sludge
it pools, dirty, like unresolved pain.

The concrete pipe
fires half-hearted salvoes
into the sea,
a rifle unable to master the waves
muddying its shallow mouth.

Years ago,
a girl walked there with her mother
speaking of who she might become.

Now a woman walks alone
wondering, in the shadows

how she will ever know
what it is she needs to say.

Poisoned water pisses out of the conduit,
fanning the sand beneath it
into delicate patterns.

She holds a glass shard,
smoothed by the sea.

Stands indeterminate
at the edge of the water,
waiting for the clear words to come.

Every Day

I found it in this morning's paper, online:
a story bare as the body of the 14 year old girl.
The text a scar of muted grey, no photograph,
a headline bleak as the Katlehong veld.

'Six arrested for gang rape,' it read.
The girl and her friend taken after the party
to a house in Moleleki Extension One.
Violence, cheap brandy on the breath, souring the room.

My computer hums a great divide.
Her friend identified the youths because,
the constable said, the girl claimed she could not
remember what transpired that night.

Later, in dreams, maybe, they will come to her,
the faces of the men who feared her enough,
even after they fucked her, to imprint on her skin,
the small cigarette-shaped brands of those who feel powerless.

In her shoes

We travelled by taxi into the city,
webbed in morning light.
I a girl in grown up's shoes
crossing at the green man flashing.

My mother was selling me the house she'd built.
For half-price. Her sad eyes said she was glad for me.
This gift the biggest of so many, while an ocean of morning air
washed through us, tides of years gone by, and not returning.

Time, a child, tugged at my hand,
pulling me back, as still we moved forward,
across the road to the lawyer's office.

Grahamstown Library

Memory — pale as a scar —
small girl sees wintry trees still
as sandstones standing.

almost forgotten: a scent
to the children's books,
library stairs dark as grief.

Speaking through the poem

A sea of women's faces looks up from the anthology cover,
but it is mine I seek; the small girl,
smiling through sadness from behind glass —
just a photograph on a dressing table now.

This night, rain dripping like tears from the eaves
and my breath sounding, as waves do, entering me, leaving me,
I write, to accept it, solitude, solitude, accept.

Doppelganger

You are my terrible twin.
We were knotted together even as I slipped,
womb-blinded, from the darkness into light,
the cord severed.

We will always be as Janus was,
selves torn between the ancient face
that looks forward from the doorway
and the young one that looks back,
into the shadows,
different sides of the same shiftless coin.

No closeness has ever felt further.
No mirror glitters so cruelly
with false promise
as the one you hold up for me.

It is because you left me,
that I cannot relinquish you,
must carry you like a dog-eared copy
of a sad book I do not want to read.

Pushed over by a careless hand,
choices tumble like dominoes, maze-makers,
spilling into a future I struggle to claim.

When I was small you laid your head
upon my chest, listening to my heart
as if it were the only sound in the world.

Now, from far, I trace your faint presence
as a cardiac monitor might mimic a waning pulse,
needle ready to mark a small final
end point on the spooling graph paper.

Lucky Bean Necklace

To write: wear scarlet
seeds threaded through centres black,
girl, stick out your neck

From the sea

You, poet, alone, immobile, at your keyboard,
the night sighing, a stranger at your back.
You wrestle the anger of the invisible,
lay it down.
Stop picking at the scabs
that make you mute. Look around.
Poets shoal within reach,
breaching the surface.

Other Poetry titles by Modjaji Books

Fourth Child by Megan Hall

Life in Translation by Azila Talit Reisenberger

Please, Take Photographs by Sindiwe Magona

Burnt Offering by Joan Metelerkamp

Strange Fruit by Helen Moffett

Oleander by Fiona Zerbst

The Everyday Wife by Phillippa Yaa de Villiers

Removing by Melissa Butler

Piece Work by Ingrid Anderson

missing by Beverly Rycroft

These are the Lies I told you by Kerry Hammerton

The Suitable Girl by Michelle McGrane

Difficult Gifts by Dawn Garisch